UNSHACKLED

Stories of Hope, Triumph and Wholeness

Joyce M.H. Samuels
Literary Lead

Printed in the United States of America

First Printing, 2016

King James Version (KJV) by Public Domain

New International Version (NIV) Holy Bible, New International
Version®, NIV® Copyright © 1973, 1978, 1984, 2011 by
Biblica, Inc. ® Used by permission. All rights reserved
worldwide

New Living Translation Scripture quotations marked (NLT) are
taken from the Holy Bible, New Living Translation, copyright ©
1996, 2004, 2007 by Tyndale House Foundation. Used by
permission of Tyndale House Publishers, Inc., Carol Stream,
Illinois 60188.

ISBN: 978-0-692-77200-3

FOREWORD

By
Natasha Aughtry

Have you ever been so bound that you could hardly move from one moment to the next? So bound that you were ashamed to even look yourself in the eye, knowing the indescribable amount of pain and brokenness that you carried from day to day? Bound so tightly by the weight of life or pass trauma to the point that it even hurt to breathe?

Chains come in many shapes and sizes. Oftentimes a person is wrapped and wound up well before they even know there is a problem or an issue. You see, there is a power in chains that often is not truly recognized until the last piece is placed in position. Heartache, brokenness, fear, unspeakable pains and even past traumas can form chains that seem unbreakable and immovable. Each link of the chain holds a memory and tells a story that can even make the strongest person break. Often held together by tears, unforgiveness, abuse and many other forms of bondage.

So how do you find true freedom? How do you undue years of pain and torment? How can one find healing when healing seems so unattainable? In Unshackled, you will see many gain true freedom and victory over the very chains that attempted to destroy their lives. Unshackled will share many testimonies of triumph, hope, determination and an unshakable faith in the power of God. Searching for true freedom? Unshackled is the book for you!

DEDICATION

We dedicate this book to the women who have been broken, in bondage or held captive but now walk in their new found liberty. We salute you for not allowing the troubles of this world and the storms that you endured, to keep you from grabbing Christ's hand when you needed Him to break you free from the chains of life!

INTRODUCTION

Unshackled is defined as to be free or delivered from confinement, violence, danger, or evil. It is the act of releasing a person from a state of physical, mental or spiritual captivity. Being unshackled is something that the person who is held captive longs for but knows that freedom will only take place when their savior finds them and emancipates them from whatever has them bound.

In Unshackled, you will read ten accounts of women who were knowingly or unknowingly bound by sickness, drugs, depression, generational curses, failed marriages, unsuccessful singleness, etc. These women fought through situations until they discovered that their life meant more than the state of bondage that they were in. They all arrived at the same conclusion that Christ who died for their sins had freed them and wanted to give them the opportunity to receive this freedom.

As you read these accounts of hope, triumph and wholeness, you will gasp, you will cry, you will cheer and you will see how much God loved these women to set them free to tell their stories to help someone else be unshackled for God's glory.

SHARRON PETERSON
Unshackled from Spirit of Fear

I was raised by a single mother who was very strict yet a good disciplinarian. We had a very close-knit family. As a family we always celebrated every holiday together no matter what. Even as everyone got older and became independent with their families we remained close. When I was 14 my great grandmother passed away. She was the rock that held the family together. After her death, my grandmother, Inita, quickly took on the matriarch position in the family.

When my family came together we always had a great time enjoying each other's company. We had Bible study as a family. My grandmother always told us "a family that prayed together stayed together". December 2003, my stepfather died of cancer. My stepfather was the best father I could have ever had. Allen loved me like I was his biological child. I remember when I had my first child; I believe he was more excited than my parents and me. He kept my son the first night I came home from the hospital and was upset when I asked for my child. When Allen passed away, it happened rather quickly. From the time he was diagnosed with cancer till the time of his death was a matter of months. After Allen's death, our family came together as we always did in the time of need.

In 2006, my grandmother had to have a hysterectomy because she had an abnormal pap. She was concerned but I always encouraged her that there was nothing to worry about. It was a routine procedure. She had the hysterectomy with no problems. They ordered a biopsy of her cells when they performed her procedure and the results came back that she had ovarian cancer. That hit the family hard, we were not prepared at all for the devastating news. My grandmother was always full of life and she lived life to the fullest every day. After the doctors gave us the news, we had a family meeting and she told everyone she was going to fight this and become a living testimony. My grandmother went through radiation and came out victorious. She was cancer free in 2006. At some point after that my grandmother started complaining of acid reflux every time she ate, so we took her to the doctor and they stated that she should stay away from any foods that had high levels of acid. So she followed those instructions and took the medication but she was still having the same issues. She went to another doctor and they ran more test. The results were devastating; they told her that she had 6 months to live because her cancer had come back and this time it had spread to her stomach area.

She went through radiation and chemo and she didn't like the way it made her feel. She called another family meeting and she told us that she was not going to do the radiation or chemo again. If God called her home then that will be His plans. With everything that her body was going through she woke up every day and thanked God for her life. She fought her battle with so much grace it was so precious to see the transformation. When the doctors tell you that you only have 6 months to live, God will tell you when He's ready for you to come home. So God called her home January 29, 2008.

Six months after my grandmother passed my father, Pete, was diagnosed with pancreatic cancer. When I tell you that I had a "for real" conversation with God! I got down on my knees, talked and prayed with God. I told him that I could not lose my grandmother and father within the same year. You really have to be careful what you ask of God, because he will grant your prayer request when you least expect Him to. God extended the time my father was on the earth. He lost his battle to cancer February 17, 2009. My father died one year after my grandmother. I was truly a daddy's girl, so that news hit me like a ton of bricks. I was brave on the outside but on the inside I was crushed. My daddy was my superman. When I was a little girl, he always seemed to come in on his cape when I needed him the most. When you're a daddy's girl you see no wrong with your father. My father was one of my best friends. We could talk, cry and joke with one another at any time. Trust me, my Dad made some mistakes, but I love my mother for never speaking ill of my father to us. My father passed away on my youngest child's birthday. On that day I celebrate my baby's birthday and my father's life. I don't mourn his death because I know God is in control of my life.

After my dad's death I focused on raising my three children and providing for them. Death will either tear you down or bring life into prospective. For me it bought my life into prospective. I realized that life was so precious that I needed to treat everything in it like it was my last. I became closer to my family and enjoyed the time we spent together. I was working and went back to school to become certified in reading and interpreting EKG's, so I could provide a better life for my children. Life was good. We had a roof over our heads, food and clothes. We attended church because I was raised to always bring your children to Christ. We were living life to the fullest then here comes death knocking on my family door again.

This time my two great-uncles, my oldest and youngest uncles, were diagnosed with liver cancer. My uncles were two peas and a pod. When you saw one you always knew the other wasn't far behind. They were so close that they passed away within three days of each other. They did everything together even in death. So this was another blow to our family, having to deal with two deaths at the same time. However, God kept us together and got us through this overwhelming time as a family. We knew and would tell others the only way that we got through the death of our family members, was with God's help.

I always asked God why He was taking everyone that meant so much to me from me. I don't understand why all this death is going on in my family. Then I heard God say to me "I need your family's attention and I will keep taking them away until the family listens". With death came a learning experience for me. With every death I became closer and closer to God, because He's the only one who could get me through those sleepless nights. I talked to everyone about how I was feeling and the only response that I would receive was, "I'm sorry for your loss, if there is anything that I can do for you please let me know." I wanted to say can you bring my family back? That's the only thing that I wanted at that time.

Soon after, I was at work one day and went to lunch and met this guy. We became friends very quickly. I wasn't looking to meet anyone at the time but I always believe that people came into your life for a reason, season or lifetime. This guy was nice and I believe at that time that he was a good distraction from everything that was going on in my life. We began dating and everything was wonderful in the beginning. Then I was hit by a car and broke my leg. I had to have emergency surgery. To this day, I have a metal rod and pins in my leg. I was struck by the car as I was walking across the street and all I could think about was what would happen to my children if something happened to me. I began to pray that God please spare my life.

My recovery was rough. I couldn't bare weight on my right leg at all. I decided then to let my boyfriend move in with my kids and me so he could help me with my recovery. My mom didn't like anything about him. Usually when my mother doesn't like a male I introduce her to, I leave him alone. Yet this was so different this time and I didn't understand why. When I let him move in to my house my life turned upside down. My mother told me that he was very controlling but I reassured her that I was not easily controllable.

The first time this man put his hands on me, I was shocked. I had never been in an abusive relationship. I tried to leave but he took my keys. I had gotten to the point where I wanted to kill him just to get away from him. One night while he was asleep, I got my daughter and me out the house in the middle of the night and went to my aunt's home. I was safe because he didn't know where I was. He called my phone every day and even had his sister to call me to see why I left my house.

Once again, I had never experienced abuse in a relationship before. I'm a strong willed woman and I kept telling myself no one would run me out of my house. I wanted him out of my house and I was going home to throw him out. My family didn't want me to go back home, but against their wishes I returned. So much was going on in my family. At that time, my mother's sister was diagnosed with colon cancer and all my family was in Philadelphia at The Cancer Institute with my aunt while she was going through surgery.

I returned to my home while my family was away. He knew that they were out of town. I woke up one morning and he tried to kill me. He beat me so bad that I just knew my daughter would come home and find me dead. It took everything in me to keep myself from passing out, because I knew if I passed out he would have killed me. When my daughter came in from school and saw my face she asked what happened. He told her that we were playing and I fell off the bed and hit my face on the floor. My daughter knew it was a lie, she wanted to help but she didn't know how because he was so controlling. He would listen to every conversation I had with her. The next morning I told my daughter when she arrived to school to inform her teacher that her mother was in trouble at home and to please send the police because she was in danger at home. I just knew help would come as soon as she arrived at school. However, when my daughter left for school my abuser told her that whatever I had said to her that I changed my mind. My child didn't know what to do because he had confused her.

My aunt wasn't doing well. When my mother would call to give me updates he would give me the phone and take it away right after I hang up. He was in control of everything that was going on in my home. I couldn't understand how I had falling into such an abusive relationship. I was always so strong-willed! After my attack he was afraid that I was going to try to escape so he drank a case of energy drinks. The abuse lasted for almost three days before he finally went to sleep. When he finally crashed, I grabbed my child and my phone and we got out as fast as we could. I had to hide in my neighborhood because he had my car keys. I called one of my aunts and she came and got my daughter and me. While with my aunt, I called my mother and she took me straight to the hospital and we called the police to make a report. While all this was happening my Aunt Parthenia was at the Cancer Institute fighting for her life.

I received clearance from the ER to be released and I went to Philadelphia to the hospital to visit my aunt. I came in the room and I told her that I was safe and I wasn't going back to my house that I was there with her. She couldn't speak to me but she nodded her head in acknowledgment. That was the last conversation I had with my aunt. She passed the next day. Cancer had struck my family again. I asked God again why my family; why are you taking so many from us? What are we not doing as a family that you are taking so many? After the funeral services for my aunt were over I did not go home. I was so upset that my Ex was on the run and he was going to get away with what he had done to me.

He would call often telling me how sorry he was and how much he loved me but I didn't believe a word that he said. Although I knew he was lying, I never let him know that because I wanted him to reveal where he was hiding. So I came up with a plan. I called and told him that all was forgiven and I wanted to be back with him no matter what anyone said. I was trying to set him up so that I could get him arrested. I had a friend that was a police officer and my plan was to drive in the district where he worked. My officer friend was going to pull me over and arrest my Ex because of his outstanding warrant. My plan didn't quite work as I had planned. I ended up being with him for at least another three days and it was torture for me. Thank God for my mother who knew something went wrong. She called the police to come to my house and arrested him. That was the best day of my life!

He was charged with felony assault, kidnapping and car theft. We went to court, he took a plea bargain. He is still incarcerated. One day I had a conversation with my mother and I told her that I had to forgive him for what he did to me because I couldn't let him hold the keys to my life. I forgave him for me. My mother didn't understand but she said I was strong to forgive.

On November 11, 2014, my mother, Claudette suddenly became ill. Her aorta had a tear in it and she had to be rushed into emergency open-heart surgery. Before she went into surgery she told me that if she didn't make it don't worry because she would be with her heavenly father. My mother passed on December 4, 2014. That was the hardest day of my life. My mom and I were best friends but that crazy relationship that I was in put such a strain on our friendship.

Forgiveness is a matter of the heart for me so I can have peace in my life. I asked God that whatever storms He took me through to let me use it for good, to let my testimony help someone else. I was abused and all of my family was dying, but God is still in control of my life and I just want to say Thank you to Him for breaking the shackles of fear from my life.

VALERIE JOHNSON-PHILSON
Unshackled from Addiction

When I was nine years old, I smoked cigarettes. I would take my lunch money at least one day a week and buy a pack of Benson and Hedges or Kool cigarettes. I would sit on my babysitter's front porch and smoke while she was in the house watching her soap operas on television. A year later, I was chain-smoking almost an entire pack of cigarettes and became ill. I was so nauseous, and had to hide it from the babysitter and my parents. That nauseous feeling made me never want to pick up another cigarette in my life.

When I was 12 years old, I began smoking pot with my grandfather. My parents would give me lunch money for the week and I would take that money and buy me a nickel bag a few days a week before going to school. That was my routine until I was about 15 years old.   At the age of 15, my Aunt Jessie Samuels-Wells, invited me to Unity Church of God In Christ. I fell in love with the singing, dancing, and the music. I could not believe this was a church service. I continued to go to church and eventually joined. I gave my life to Christ and was eventually licensed as a junior missionary. I also sang on the youth choir as well as the Triumph Choir.

At the age of 17, I met my husband, Craig, and we began dating. I fell in love with him. I got pregnant but miscarried a little girl. After hanging out with Craig and his friends, I was introduced to PCP. I smoked PCP off and on until I was 20 years old.

When I turned 18, Craig and I moved into an apartment together in SE, Washington, DC. After living together for a couple of years, Craig and I began to hang out with people that were abusing crack cocaine. I became addicted for 15 years. I actually started using crack cocaine when I was nine months pregnant with my oldest son in 1985. I started spending $50 every Friday. I had my son December 9, 1985, and thank God he was not addicted. After having my son, my habit became more intense. I began to use crack more than on Fridays. I was smoking almost every day. April 16, 1987, I had a daughter who was also not addicted but as time went on, I continued to smoke every day. December 8, 1988, I had a son and on November 16, 1990, I had my last son and they thankfully were both not addicted to the drugs I had been putting in my system.

After I had my four children, I started smoking eight balls ($250 street value) and quarters ($500 street value) of cocaine at a time. I never lost custody of my children. All of my children graduated high school on time. My oldest son joined the Army Reserve where he is still enlisted. My children have their own families and are all doing well. I have five grandchildren and expecting another later this year.

During this time period, I could not keep a job, but did work off and on. Because I could not keep a job, I signed up to receive a welfare check and food stamps for at least 8 years. My husband worked full time and was a drug dealer on the side. He was one of the few drug dealers that provided me with crack. We also went to drug spots to purchase when we needed to.

During my fifteen years of addiction, I continued to attend church on Sundays. I did not always want to go, but my stepfather, Dennis Mack (Bud) would call and tell me, "be ready in the morning." I would get ready for church, even if I had been up all night, as I did not want to disappoint Bud. Every Sunday, I would get in the prayer line and ask God to deliver me from crack cocaine.

I believe that because I gave my life to Christ; when I backslid, God never took his hands off of me. He allowed the enemy to keep my mind wanting to use drugs, but did not allow the enemy to make me a prostitute or a thief. On the other hand, I would lie to get money for drugs. I cannot count the times that I told my parents and grandparents stories to get money. I would make up stories like, my kids have a field trip; or they have to take pictures; or a utility is about to be turned off, etc. I would also pawn any electronics; bikes; and jewelry that I had at any given moment to get a hit.

During this period of my life, I had a few incidents where I could have been placed in jail, but again, I believe God had a plan for my life that did not include jail. I had a checking account that was closed and I would go to the Giant and Safeway Food stores and write checks for my food and get at least $50 cash back. I did that until Giant Food took me to court to get their money back.

When I went to court, the judge could not believe that I owed Giant over $1,000. The judge allowed me to pay a little bit at a time until the bill was paid off and I made sure I paid it off.

Another incident that I should have been locked up for was when my grandfather's girlfriend had a man driving my grandfather's vehicle and I saw them. I made them pull over. We had words and I told my husband to take the car, because it was a stick shift and I couldn't drive it. My friend Gary then drove my husband's van and ran the stop sign right in front of the police. The police pulled us over and Gary jumped in the back of the van and I hopped into the driver's seat. The police approached me asking for my driver's license and registration. While the police went back to his car, a call came in that a woman had car jacked this lady and I had weapons in the van. It was not completely true. I had no weapons and I did not actually car jack her. I was in a van not the car that she was driving. The police handcuffed me and read me my rights. They kept me handcuffed for about 20 minutes. They interviewed her and she lied on me. After the Captain finished interviewing the lady, he came to interview me and when I told him what happened, they took the handcuffs off of me. The police locked my friend up, because he had a warrant. The police would not let me leave driving the van, so the police drove me to my grandfather's house to verify that I was his granddaughter and they let me go. I had my husband bring the car back later that night.

After being on welfare for about 8 years, Social Services decided to implement a program to make women go to school if they wanted to stay in the system. I went to PG College and received several certificates, while still abusing drugs. In the program, I met a young lady that wanted me to rob banks and also go to a club and strip to make good money. I thank God that he did not allow me to go down that path. The young lady was working as a Contractor at Housing and Urban Development (HUD). She would tell me how she had a job making $100 a day and I asked her for the contact information.

In 1991, I became a Contractor for HUD. I maintained my crack cocaine habit and went to work. It was a hard job, but again, I believe the Lord had His arms around me. I worked in many offices at HUD, but I did 10 years off and on in the Labor and Employee Relations (LERD) office as a Secretary. This office was family oriented. We all cared for each other and worked well together. There was a lady in the office that was a preacher and she wanted me to get my life right with the Lord, so much so, that she would take my children and me with her for Bible Study on Tuesday nights. My children and I would also go to her church for special services.

While working in LERD, my husband's job sold the company and he got a severance check for approximately $80,000. One day on my lunch break, he picked me up after getting some money from the check. I told the HR Specialist that relieved me that I was going to lunch. I showed back up to work a week later.

My mom told me that my job had called her house looking for me. They were worried that something had happened, as I had never left for days without calling the office to let them know I would be out. When I went back to work a week later, the Director called me in her office. I lied and told her that I had gotten locked up when I went to lunch. She sent me to the EAP office where I could seek counseling. I was so thankful they did not terminate me. As a contractor they could have requested someone else.

On one particular day in 2000, I had been up all night getting high. The drug dealer had come and I bought what drugs he had on him. I sent him to get a quarter. While waiting on him to come back, my husband told me that no more crack was coming in the house. He informed me that if I continued using crack, he would leave. I told him, that I was ready to give it up. When the drug dealer came back with the drugs, I had to tell him that was okay. It was one of the hardest tasks I had to endure. I know that it had to be God that used my husband to tell me no more drugs, because to this day I've never used any more drugs. Crack is one of the hardest drugs to get clean from, and I have never been to a doctor, rehab or any of addiction meetings. 15 years later I am still clean.

I was licensed to preach the gospel in 2008. I graduated from Lancaster Bible College in August 2014, and I am currently in Seminary pursuing a Master's Degree in Leadership. I am also a GS-13 in the Federal Government. God allowed me to go through a life of drug use to be able to let people know that because you use drugs it is not the end of the road. You can stop and be someone. Everyone will not get unshackled from drugs as I did, but if it takes for a person to go to rehab, it can be done. You don't have to stay shackled! If you trust in God, He will UNSHACKLE you!!!

LINDA D. PARKER
Unshackled from Myself

I thank my Lord and Savior Jesus Christ, for His grace and mercy. I haven't always been so thankful, going on about my way, establishing my own righteousness. However, a few years ago it hit me when I had nowhere else to turn. It's funny when you come to realize you have been wrong and you have no one to confide in, but you know it is all in God's timing. He knows we will turn to Him, so I fell on my knees and confessed to Jesus Christ that I was sorry for the way I had lived my life; a life that didn't belong to me any anyway. I was bought with a price, purchased with my Saviors' blood, which was sent by His father. Today I am thankful; I appreciate life. I try to commit to my creator and His Son who redeemed me unto the father. Now I can say there is meaning to life. I can awake and know God gave me another chance to love and to live on purpose according to His righteousness and His glory. When I began to trust God, I began to read His word and my days began to have meaning.

In 2003, God gave me a vision while I visited my niece in Arizona. I was in her home alone one day cleaning my room and the spirit hit me and that's when God began to show me how filthy I was. The vision was a black pot boiling gold and as it began to boil; black smoke rolled over the top to the floor. God was showing me He was cleaning me up and I began to cry and weep. As the vision continued I was still wiping myself and crying and asking for forgiveness and the Lord began to talk to me and I could hear Him saying, "never walk this way again. I am cleaning you up and the things you did, they don't belong to you anymore. The things you did, you did to please man and yourself. I am refining you and you will begin to hear my voice all the more. I want you to use this as your testimony to edify my people, to establish the Kingdom for which you are called by my name and the spirit left me." I tried to get it back. I tried to feel that feeling again but the spirit was gone and I was never the same. Like Moses made excuses that he couldn't talk, but when he knew God was with him his confidence grew and his faith led him to do whatever God told him to do. We have to make sure it is God who told us to do it.

The heaviness left me, the load became light and the light that was once dark became brighter revealing the darkest place of my life. The more I read God's word, the more my eyes became open and something on the inside of me began to change. I began to have more compassion for God's people. I began to love myself and in my heart I began to guard what I would let in. I began to understand more according to the word.

The word of God opens up a new understanding in the way that nothing else can. His words had new meaning for me. When I read the Bible it speaks to me. I believe that is the difference of just reading. But when you hunger and thirst for the word, it gives new meaning and new understanding to you. The more I read God's word the more I yearn for it and understand life better. I eat better, exercise more, my prayer life is good and the words are forever in my life. Things began to open up for me in my circumstances and I continue to allow God to work things out. I don't worry anymore because God will do just what He said He would do. He said He would never "leave me nor forsake me". He said "Seek Ye First the Kingdom of God and all His righteousness and all these things (the needs I have) will be added to me."

I believe that in addition to studying the word, you should have a great church home, surrounded by people who love you and care about you the way that God does. You should also have a pastor, one who loves God and God's people.

Jesus was fully complete in God and with us being heir to Jesus Christ we are fully complete as well. As we abide in His love we must stay connected to Him and to one another. We are our brother's keeper. We must love ourselves as well as our neighbor.

In Galatians 5:22 speaks of the fruit of the spirit being love, joy, peace, long-suffering gentleness, and goodness. Faith, meekness, temperance against such there is no law because it is the realm of God. When we begin to operate in them we are in the realm of Kingdom living. Galatians 5:25 says if we live in the spirit we learn the things God desires of us. Operating in the spirit and have faith to work out our soul salvation. This will help ourselves to help someone else that is coming out of bondage.

See, we don't have to be behind bars to be in bondage. We don't have to be in prison or in captivity to be in bondage. I was in bondage to my lying, with my stealing, and with my fornication.

I was not sure if I was going to see my way out of it but that was satan deceiving me. God ministered to me through His spirit, "if I am for you, who can be against you. Greater is He who is in you, than he that is in the world. I created the whole universe. I even created you; so don't fear cause I am that I am." My testimony is that God called me out of those things. He led me into faith. He asked me to walk out into the deep because He was never going to leave me or allow me to fall. God told me to trust Him and have faith because He was faithful to me.

God created us for Himself, and we belong to Him for his righteousness. Learn of Him and be the light so others can see Him through us, your neighbor may not go to church but are watching us to be an example. We are the only bible they may read. Love one another the way God created us to love. Our testimony draws other people to Christ.

God called me out of my bondage and His word began to manifest within me and the outside began to look like the inside. That's the way it is with God. If you abide in Him and He abides in you there is security. Jesus is the vine and we are the branches. The substance we get from the vine keeps us fruitful. I have learned to abide within the vine, connecting to Jesus and He is within me and I am fruitful and bearing the fruit of the Spirit.

So sisters and brothers, know this, I will soar like an eagle, fly high above my trouble because of the creator. He is holy and I must be holy too. God is the head of the church and we are the body of Christ. We are fully complete with what God intended us to be in Christ. We are with Christ in a relationship and along with the gift we inherited through Him who died on the cross for us. But on that third day, He rose and all power belonged to Him. He wrestled with the death angel and took the sting out of death. When He assented back to the Father, He sent a comforter back to us and it gave us power over the enemy. We are disciples now and God is using us to work our Faith to bring His people out of bondage. A call to repentance, so we can do a work for Him; a work that will cause us to gain a seat in Glory. God loves us and His purpose is that we do His will. When God restored me, I knew it was not just for me to keep it to myself. It is to be used as a testimony so others will know if He did it for me, He would do the same for them. Just like Peter, when he received the comforter, he stood up and preached the Gospel of Jesus Christ and three thousand people was added to the church. God called me into the ministry and I am proud to proclaim the Gospel to everyone who wants to be called, "Saints of God". Even though, I will receive a crown, I want others to be unshackled by God, too!

YVONNE LOVELADY
Unshackled from My Past

I can remember bits and pieces of my childhood. I remember being the happiest little girl from Arkansas then relocating to Detroit, Michigan. Our family moved to Waukegan, Illinois for a short time then to Zion, Illinois. I could remember going to Good News Club every Tuesday after school when I was in the 4th grade. As I grew older, I felt that there was something missing in my life. I didn't know what it was, just a feeling. There was a night when my friends and I were supposed to go on a church trip to Indiana but it rained that evening and we decided not to go. Later that night we received sad news that the bus was in an accident. Three of my friends were badly hurt and two were killed. That could have been me on that bus. God spared my life.

Through my junior high years I kept very busy with sports. I love running track and playing basketball. It kept me away from home a lot. During that time my mom and dad were going through a separation. There was so much verbal, physical, and mental abuse that I had encountered in my home for many years. Yet, I was so torn apart when my mom and dad separated then divorced. I didn't have that father figure in the home like a daughter needed. I missed my dad a lot. I graduated from high school and went on to college. My first year in college I conceived my first son, but I had no intention of getting married to his father. Years passed by and I had three more children. I wondered about life; realizing that no one had ever talked to me about the birds and the bees. I was just having babies after babies and no direction. I can remember after my second child the father and I agreed to go and get an abortion. I remember going to Chicago and getting prepared. The nurse said, "Are you sure about this?" I said, "yes." I was giving an ultrasound to see how far along I was in the pregnancy. The craziest thing was, the nurse did not see a baby. I knew I was pregnant. I went back home and months went by. My stomach was getting bigger and bigger. Pregnant again.

The relationship I was in had the same characteristics of my parents' relationship, verbally and mentally abusive. For 18 years of that relationship I allowed my children to go through it all. What type of mother was I? I wondered was my life always going to be this way. When I thought my situation was going to change for the good it didn't. I stayed in that relationship because I worked two jobs and was attending college part time. Wondering who is going to look after my children while I worked and attended school. Finally, I just got sick and tired, and I asked, "is there something better? My life has to change."

In April 2006, The Lord spoke to my heart calling me by my name. "Yvonne" He called. It's like He took me away from my unhealthy relationship of 18 years. I was on my own with my four children and the Lord began to deal with me where I was. Stripping off the old so I could receive my healing. I could not understand why I was a people pleaser. I would always please others before myself. Everyone else came first. I was all about my children and other people. I'd always kept myself on the back burner. All I wanted to do at this point was to assist my children in graduation from high school and then onto college. I was so used by relationships; I was always in covenant with people but they were never in covenant with me. I was that person who would help any and every one when they were in need.

I was searching for covenant relationships but really did not know who I was. I would allow people to define who I was. Telling me what I should do or be. I started to believe in others who I was. Moreover, I would always be in fear, fear of the unknown, life, people or what others may say, stepping out and doing something new. I was in so much lack and poverty. I can say I am a giver but I never saw the harvest. My children were always taken care of, yet I feared my children would not go to college. I recall a friend telling me, "Yvonne you always have faith, you just didn't know you had it."

Many people, even family members often talked about me. However, that friend introduced me to deliverance. She invited me to attend a church in the Chicago area and all I can say was that service changed my life. I started attending church. There was urgency in my spirit to change and to live right. Once I knew who God was I was obedient to Him. Everything I heard in my spirit I would do. I was truly sold out for God. Every time I would obey Him, He blessed me. That had been the first time, in a long time; I had gotten my joy back. God would speak and I would obey. Even now, out of all my obedience, He continues to bless my children as well. I sow, give, and help others. All of my children went to college and are now living independently. That was my fear. I did not want them to struggle like I did. I wanted them to succeed.

Many people, even family members, often talked about me. However, that friend introduced me to deliverance. She invited me to attend a church in the Chicago area and all I can say was that service changed my life. I started attending church. There was urgency in my spirit to change and to live right. Once I knew who God was I was obedient to Him. Everything I heard in my spirit I would do. I was truly sold out for God. Every time I would obey Him, He blessed me. That had been the first time, in a long time; I had gotten my joy back. God would speak and I would obey. Even now, out of all my obedience, He continues to bless my children as well. I sow, give, and help others. All of my children went to college and are now living independently. That was my fear. I did not want them to struggle like I did. I wanted them to succeed.

My deliverance was a process that I surrendered to. I knew it was time to get down to the core and start working on me. I was able to be totally transparent with the Lord. I really wanted to be delivered and set free from my past and bloodline, generational curses. I could not understand why I had put up so many walls and really didn't trust people. People would try to embrace me with hugs but I couldn't let anyone get next to me. This went on for years.

During this intense deliverance process, the Lord showed me an Uncle but for months I didn't understand why he was in my spirit. The Lord then revealed to me I was molested at a very early age. That was a big block of my childhood in which I had suppressed. That is why I didn't let others get next to me. I did not know what to think or do as God revealed it to me. The first thing I did was forgive him. I spoke to the Lord and said, "Lord forgive him for what he did to me in the past." I started to cry and released him. I went to visit him a year ago. I was able to hug him with love. My heart was right. I even took it to another level. I went back and forgave all the others who did me wrong and talked about me. Those who mistreated me and those I mistreated. What a big release! Like a burden was lifted off my back. I was able to see those friends who talked about me and did me wrong. I was able to embrace them with the love of God. It was not about me. Some embraced me with a hug some didn't and that was okay. Until my natural father and me were reunited, my heavenly Father loved me and stood in the gap. The Lord was dealing with me one step at a time.

Deliverance also took place with me concerning the "pleasing people spirit" I was allowing myself to say yes to people in the past. I was allowing myself to please God rather than man. It felt really good! I don't feel the pressure to perform anymore. It's okay to say NO! The Lord was now showing me the way He sees me. I had allowed others to define who I was. The Lord put in my spirit I was perfectly made in His image. I would always ask the Lord let me see myself the way you see me and I started to believe it. He even let me see myself dressing in nice gorgeous clothing the way He sees me. At this point, the Lord had rescued me and made me whole again. My heart was so broken, tattered and torn from friends, family and church people, simply because I did not fit their profile. I was always the outcast. Now God has placed me in a new circle of friends who I can say are Covenant. I don't have to worry about not fitting in. My new relationships don't use me or talk about me behind my back. They are there to push me in the right direction. I can tell the difference and it feels good. They are able to cultivate my gifts, gifts I didn't even know I possessed. The relationships came at the right divine time. I no longer have the spirit of fear. God has been working on me in that area. I was so afraid of becoming who God wanted me to become. He has used an awesome woman of God, Apostle Candace Ford to assist me in this area. I met her two years ago at a church meeting in Chicago. After she preached, she said come here young lady. The Lord said, "get rid of all things in your home that are five years and older." Then she began to say the Lord said, "He is going to change your wardrobe and friends; new relationships." At the very end, she said the Lord said, "you have six weeks to get your website up and going." I attended a few more of her events and I started to step out of the agreement of fear. I just started to step out of fear and did what I was supposed to do. My ministry is called, *Love & Care Outreach International Ministry*. We assist the homeless in various communities. The more I stepped out, the less I feared. I started to travel more, trying new things, and going to different restaurants. I was breaking free! Not fearing what people would say or think anymore. Now I can say I am the happiest person on the face of the earth. As I looked back on my life it is true, I don't look like what I've been through. I know my latter is going to be my greater. The Lord rescued and made me whole again. He gave me hope, triumph and provision. I am who He called me to be. I don't have to look back on my past. My past is a reminder what He delivered me from and brought me out of. He gave me faith to believe the impossible. All the heartbreak, and everything I've been through, was for my making. I am not afraid to share what God did for me to others. All I can say," My testimony today is:

- I have joy and a peace of mind
- I know who I am, because God says who I am
- I am an overcomer
- I no longer fear the unknown. Love cast out fear
- I am the head and not the tail
- I no longer let people define who I am
- I am healed
- I am delivered
- I am set free from my past
- I am no longer a people pleaser. I please my heavenly father
- I am in covenant with the right relationships

- God supplies all my needs and my children (Julian, Antoine, Jeremy, Candace and Jada)
- I am made whole again
- I no longer live in lack or poverty
- I am a giver
- I am living a long life, me and my children

I am not where I use to be, I'm moving forward. All I can say is if God can deliver, heal and set me free from my past, He can do it for you. You have to trust Him. Everything you need, give it all to Him. He will come to unshackle you. I was drowning, He came and broke my chains.

I want to encourage those who are reading this right now. If you are struggling with something from your past or present and you are trying to break away, turn it over to the Lord. You may have not because you asked not. I had to give all my broken chains and shackles over to the Lord. He healed me. It was a process and did not happen overnight. But He did it! If He can do it for me, He can do it for you! He has restored my past. Every chain that tried to break me, the Lord stepped in and used those chains to link me back together.

CHIKITA BROWN MANN
Unshackled from Infertility

Infertility. Miscarriage. Two words NO woman ever wants to hear or to experience. Those two words evoke different emotions –guilt, despair, shame, hurt, anger, embarrassment, and feelings of being incomplete. You constantly question your womanhood. Well this is how my story begins.

I was married at the age of 26. Truthfully, I wasn't concerned about getting pregnant within the first year of marriage, but after the second year, I did start to wonder why I hadn't conceived. After scheduling a visit with my gynecologist, some diagnostic testing was performed and it was revealed that I had very low progesterone levels. Progesterone was prescribed to help regulate my menstrual cycles and increase my chances of conceiving. When pregnancy did not occur after three months, my gynecologist suggested fertility medications.

I was not pleased with the recommendation, but I took the prescription home yet never got it filled. Instead I went to the Word of God. I studied the lives of Sarah and Hannah. I also bought the book, "Supernatural Childbirth" by Jackie Mize and read it from cover to cover. I was determined to believe God for a child. One day as I was reading about Sarah, I prayed, "God, if you have the power to enable a 90 year old woman to conceive and have a child, I know you can heal me and enable me to conceive." Shortly after that prayer, I found out I was pregnant with my first child, a daughter. It was an uneventful pregnancy and delivery. My husband and I were overjoyed!!

When my daughter was three years old, I became pregnant again. We were elated. Great timing to have another child and we felt this was another opportunity for God to get the glory from our previous challenge with infertility. When I was 6 weeks, a preliminary ultrasound was done to confirm how far along I was. Shockingly, there was a faint heartbeat. The ultrasound technician attempted to console me with a suggestion that I was not as far along with the pregnancy as I thought I was. But I was heartbroken. How could this be happening to me? Two weeks later, I miscarried. I was devastated, bewildered, and stunned. Even though I was only 8 weeks along, the loss was nothing I had ever experienced in my life. Three days, after the miscarriage I was listening to "I Will Trust" by Donnie McClurkin. That song ministered to me greatly and still does. I cried for almost two weeks. I just could not understand how I could have had a miscarriage. I was a tither and I had been faithful in serving in ministry. I found solace and understanding from other women in my church, but I still felt diminished and questioned my womanhood. Two months later, I conceived again. What joy!!! At six weeks, however, I began spotting and was instructed by my obstetrician/gynecologist to go to the emergency room. At the emergency room, I began to converse with the ultrasound technician and discovered that she had had multiple miscarriages, but believed God to have a child. Believe it or not – I began ministering to her. Yes – I was miscarrying and began to minister to her. I recommended that she do the following:

1. Prepare her body to become pregnant. Be meticulous about the foods she was consuming, as she needed to strengthen her body and nourish the child while she was pregnant.

2. Get the book "Supernatural Childbirth". Read it over and over.

3. Speak to her body that she would conceive and carry the baby full term.

Unfortunately, I miscarried again. I began to retreat and avoid other women. I was embarrassed again. Two months later, I became pregnant again. I was meticulous about my eating and avoided strenuous activity. I miscarried a third time. My husband suggested that we not try for another child, as he did not like to see the pain I was enduring. Yet, I was adamant through my pain, disappointment and tears, my daughter would have a sibling. If something were to happen to my husband, or me I did not want her in the world alone.

In order to help me cope with the miscarriages, my husband planned a cruise for us to get away. In the airport returning from the cruise, I remember looking at a baby in a stroller and silently began to cry. I knew somehow I would conceive again and carry a child full-term. I had done it before. Also my obstetrician/gynecologist had some extensive blood testing done and it was discovered that I was severely deficient in folic acid and I was prone to developing blood clots. These two factors were the reasons why I was having the miscarriages. Finally some answers! I knew how to pray specifically for healing and I also knew that God was a healer. He watches over His Word to perform it. I honestly felt rejuvenated and ready for the fight because I knew how to fight.

Yes – I conceived again. As soon as I realized that I was pregnant, my obstetrician/gynecologist prescribed extra folic acid and baby aspirin to prevent miscarriages. I carried the baby full-term and had a healthy baby boy. Twenty-two months later, I had another healthy boy. Both pregnancies uneventful! Look at God!

After my second son, I had to be admitted due to some complications. While I was in the emergency room, a woman walked into my room. We both exclaimed at the same time, "I know you!" It was the ultrasound technician that I met and ministered to during my second miscarriage. She proceeded to tell me that after our conversation, she did exactly what I had instructed her to do and she had a three-year-old son. The pregnancy was uneventful. Her doctor was amazed that she carried the baby full term and Noah was a very wise little boy. Isn't God awesome?! He had given her one son and I now had two sons. I gave at a most inconvenient time in my life and God honored it.

When I was going through the miscarriages, NEVER would I have imagined that God would get any glory out of that time in my life. But He has! I have had the opportunity to minster to other women and support them through their trials with infertility and miscarriages.

I learned through my trials that isolation only intensifies feelings of guilt, shame and embarrassment. It is the subtle tactics of the enemy that make you think that no one understands what you are going through. He makes you think that you are not a whole woman if you are having issues with infertility and miscarriages. As a believing woman, you are a unique enemy to satan as you have the ability to bring life into the world; a life that you can influence to be another warrior of God to tear down the enemy's camp. Withdrawal is not just to friends and family, but also within the family – specifically, the husband. The enemy comes to steal, kill and destroy. Infertility and miscarriages have been known to cause a great deal of stress in marriages, and sadly, can be contributing factors in couples getting a divorce. When a woman encounters infertility and miscarriages, it can be easy to push the husband away. The husband is usually the forgotten person with these issues. In times like these, the power of unity in prayer and faith is crucial to keeping the family together.

Another valuable lesson I learned is that a barren womb does not make a barren life. A woman does not have to settle for an unfulfilled life because of infertility. We are all complete in Christ (Colossians 2:10). Jesus came that we may have life and have it more abundantly (John 10:10). You are God's masterpiece (Ephesians 2:10) and that is not based on a woman's ability or inability to have children. God is concerned about every area of your life. Cast that care on Him.

Lastly, understand the benefit of getting evaluated by a physician. As with my case, the causes of my miscarriages were two simple factors that were easily remedied. Additionally, being able to be specific in prayer gives you the ability to pray with power and authority. According to Isaiah 55:11, the Word of God does not come back void. God is a healer and there is nothing impossible for Him. When a physician gives you options, seek God's face about His recommendations. I am a registered nurse but I am also a firm believer in God's Word. I have witnessed countless times how prayer and declaration of God's Word has trumped a physician's report. Believe the report of the Lord.

"To appoint unto them that mourn in Zion, to give unto them beauty for ashes, the oil of joy for mourning, the garment of praise for the spirit of heaviness, that they might be called trees of righteousness, the planting of the LORD, that He might be glorified."

Isaiah 61:3 KJV

"He maketh the barren woman to keep house, and to be a joyful mother of children."

Praise ye the LORD!

Psalm 113:9 KJV

TIFFANY L. JOHNSON
Unshackled from Fear, Shame and Guilt

The various Bible verses that you will read scattered throughout this excerpt are some of my favorite scriptures that pushed me to understand the woman that God wants me to become. The story that you are about to read is true and the word of God is the only thing that truly helped me become whole. Now, I confess that I'm not 100% there; nor will I ever get there until God calls me home, but as the saying goes "thank God I'm not what I used to be." Selah

"*P*.U.S.H. *P*ass the *Pain*"

Pressure

Never in a million years did I think that the word PUSH would have such a significant meaning in my life. Life is indeed a cycle of events. *There is a time for everything, and a season for every activity under the heavens."* (Ecclesiastes 3:1 NIV) Life can also be full of unwanted pressure, and if you are not careful, the insurmountable pressure of life can literally squeeze the life out of you; to the point where you lose focus on your personal relationship with God. *"Do not worship any other god, for the LORD, whose name is Jealous, is a jealous God."* (Exodus 34:14 NIV) The year was 1991, when I decided to marry a man that I barely knew—we married in just 3 months of knowing each other. The marriage occurred in my sophomore year of college. We went to the courthouse to get married during my summer break

47

and I was barely 19 years old. My friends thought I was crazy but I thought it was love. So, I secretly married a man that was not a citizen of the United States. My parents had no idea, and I kept it a secret until well after I graduated from college. As I look back, I believed the pressure of pleasing someone else led me to the premature decision to get married at a young age. There was pressure to marry my then husband because he was not a citizen of the United States. He needed a green card as soon as possible. Once married, he had no problem with the American law because he was now a legal citizen. I know you are probably thinking how can a person pressure you into getting married? Well, before you judge me, be careful. *"Do not judge, or you too will be judged.* (Matthew 7:1 NIV) Many of my closet friends, or relatives would tell you that I'm a woman who has a passion for helping people. Therefore, I confess to you that I went into the marriage blindly, and at the time, thought I would be helping him. However, little did I realize that the marriage would hurt him, more than help him. This of course is not a way to enter a union especially a union ordained by God. *"And the two will become one flesh.' So they are no longer two, but one flesh."* (Matthew 10:8 NIV) I do not believe the marriage was necessarily a mistake but not the wisest decision under the circumstances. We were married for nearly 14 years and have two beautiful handsome sons as a result. In fact, we married in a secret ceremony in 1991; then had a church wedding in 1994 so it must have been love—or was it? Well, as the years progressed, I became increasingly unhappy about the marriage. During the course of the marriage, things began going towards a downward spiral. I definitely had the case of the "7 year and 13 year itch." The pressure to keep up *the act* as if I had the perfect marriage became increasingly stressful. Many people who looked in from the outside always said that my husband and I were the perfect match, but they never knew the turmoil I was feeling to keep my marriage afloat. I stepped outside of the marriage by looking to other people and other things to meet my needs and to try to forget my marital problems. The pressure outweighed everything and the marriage eventually ended.

Understanding

The reality and understanding of getting married at such a young age was difficult for me to comprehend. Understanding the pain that was caused when my marriage ended was such a horrible memory. For a long time, I could not understand why the marriage ended the way it did, and the things that I allowed to spiral out of control. I did not understand that not taking care of my marriage or even praying for my husband would lead to disaster. *"For I know the plans I have for you," declares the LORD, "plans to prosper you and not to harm you, plans to give you hope and a future."* (Jeremiah 29:11 NIV) For several years, I was depressed because of the failure of my marriage to the point where I thought I needed the help of a psychiatrist to help me figure out how and why I allowed my marriage to fall apart. One of my life long counselors, Dr. Deborah was extremely instrumental in helping me really understand that some of the events that occurred in my marriage were not all my fault. Dr. Deborah helped me finally realize that it takes two people to end a marriage. I was under her wing for a few years, and I thank God that she helped me push pass those stressful and painful years. *"And God will wipe away every tear from their eyes; there shall be no more death, nor sorrow, nor crying. There shall be no more pain, for the former things have passed away."* (Revelations 21:4 KJV) During my depressed years, there was weight loss, sleepless nights, psychic hotlines, and shamefully a lot of secret demons I was living with after my divorce. I had to stay strong because I had two sons who I had to raise alone. I cried many nights and talked with God about the turmoil and guilt I felt because of the failure of my marriage. As I look back during my period of understanding and the missing dots in my life at the time, I knew God was with me every step of the way. Many times, I had visions and God constantly spoke to me. One night in particular, I woke up from a dream to literally see a wooden cross with purple draping over my bed.

I can still see the vision to this day. God was so close to me back then. *"The LORD is close to the brokenhearted; he rescues those whose spirits are crushed."* (Psalms 34:18 NLT) You see despite my lack of understanding on why I was going through such a traumatic experience, God showed me during this *period* that he was with me and still with me until the end of time. *"And teaching them to obey everything I have commanded you. And surely I am with you always, to the very end of the age."* (Matthew 28:20)

Shhhh.......

I wanted my divorce to go unnoticed but that was virtually impossible because we had two sons together and most people knew who we were, plus we had to co-parent. For many years, I was embarrassed and felt like I was being ridiculed because I was divorced and had two children. During the period of isolation, God was preparing me for something greater. *"The heart of man plans his way, but the Lord establishes his steps."* (Proverbs 16:9 NLV) There were many times when I literally prayed and cried—prayed and cried, and repeated this cycle literally for months. During this time, I also lost a lot of weight, even to the point where my ring that I was wearing would slip off. I think it was right then and there that I knew I had to pay attention to what was happening to my physical appearance and to my mental state. I wanted to start my life over in a new area, so the house my husband and I shared was sold. We received a pretty significant amount of money from the sale of the house. It certainly was not the right time for me to have that kind of money in the bank because I did not make the proper decisions spending the money. I went on fancy vacations out of the country to places like Jamaica and Tortola. I also purchased lavish furniture, clothing, and jewelry. Before I knew it, the money was gone and I was back to square one. I moved to another town to get away from the stress. Yet, I found out that even after the move, the stress was still there. What I needed was a lot of God and I needed God to do a complete work in my life, especially mentally. I journaled a lot to try to get over the pain of the divorce and the aftermath. However, at times, that did not even work. Instead of dealing with the pain of divorce, I found myself dating another man who was not good for me. Although, he was not physically abusive, he was certainly mentally abusive. I did not allow myself enough time to heal from the divorce and stayed in this horrible one-sided relationship for nearly four years. I actually cared for the person a great deal but in the end I realized he was clearly not the right man for me. *"But God, who is rich in mercy, for his great love with which he loved us."* (*Ephesians 2:4* NLT) There were times, to dull the pain of my divorce, I would hang out in nightclubs to dance and drink off the pain and misery. Yes, I drank and went clubbing and then went to church the next day. I was indeed double minded because I would go to church after admittedly sinning all night. Thankfully, that period of going out to nightclubs every weekend and connecting my spirit with other spirits (dating men that were no good) ended. And, by the grace and mercy of God he brought me through that promiscuous period of time.

Hallelujah & Joy on the other side

Oh, the hallelujah, joy on the other side. I know without a shadow of a doubt that God brought me through the difficult times—the pain of the divorce was horrific. Getting myself in a few bad relationships, one after the next, following the divorce, was a mistake but God brought me through the rough times. I discovered over the course of the years, that when I talked to God and finally opened myself up to receive Him and who His word told me I was (it was process) it was then that I became completely whole. For a long period of time, I literally immersed myself in reading Bible verses. I had to do this in order to feel God's presence. I stopped going to clubs and stop listening to secular music because that put me in a mental state that I knew was not good for me. I basically decided that I needed God and all of God. I recall one night what I called "*the crying and praying cycle*", I literally told God that I needed him to bring someone in my life that truly cared about me and also has a thirst and hunger for him. "*O God, You are my God; I shall seek you earnestly; my soul thirsts for you, my flesh yearns for you, in a dry and weary land where there is no water.*" (Psalms 63:1 NSV) Hear me when I tell you my friend, when you ask God to help you with something and absolutely mean it with your heart wide open; God will indeed hear and answer. However, he will not answer if you are out of His will. As you just read, I was out of the will of God in many areas of my life but when I let go and threw my hands in the air and told God that I needed him in every area of my life, He answered all of my heart desires. Within a week after my heartfelt prayer, God brought a man in my life, who eventually became my husband. I believe my husband is a gift from the all mighty God. I never imagined that I would marry again; in fact, my prayer was not to get married but to meet a man who has a thirst for God. Well, God showed up and answered my prayers. So, whatever you are going through, my desire and prayer for you is to:

"Love the Lord your God with all your heart and with all your soul and with all your strength and with all your mind'; and, 'Love your neighbor as yourself." (Luke 27:10 NIV)

God is a man that does not lie. It is also my prayer that my story of heartbreak, my struggle to get close to God, and a new found love will encourage you to keep pressing and most of all keep pushing to be the person that God designed you to be. God understands you because He understood me. There is nothing that you cannot do or be, without the help of God.

"I press on toward the goal to win the prize for which God has called me heavenward in Christ Jesus." (Philippians 3:14 NIV). Selah

KIMBERLY DISTEFANO
Unshackled from Mental Bondage

The great philosopher and theologian, Soren Kierkegaard said, "The deepest form of despair is to choose to be another than oneself." It was only a few years ago that I was in this predicament. I don't know that I deliberately chose to be another person; however after trying for years to be everything that everyone else expected me to be, I woke up to the realization that somewhere along the way, I didn't know who I was.

It was a harsh reality thrust upon me in a harsh way. Most would say I lost myself catering to everyone else's ideas of who I was supposed to be. Yet I would say that I really couldn't remember knowing who I was. From the time I could recall, I was being shaped and formed with the purpose of fulfilling someone else's expectations, so much so, that who I was never had an opportunity to take root and grow. I was aging, maturing beyond my years but I wasn't truly growing. I was moving through life in a daze, trying to be a little bit of this and a little bit of that, with and for whom ever showed me a sliver of interest, but never quite finding peace within myself or with the myriad of strangers that came and went in my life.

Happiness was as fleeting as some of the *"situationships"* I found myself tied up in and it was situational based on what was going on in my life at any given moment. As long as I was fixing someone or catering to their preferences I could simulate happiness. Anything was preferable to pausing and taking a look at the stranger who looked back at me in the mirror. I didn't want to look too closely because I would have to admit that I didn't know who I was and didn't know how to figure it out.

I couldn't show any sign of weakness or vulnerability. In a nutshell, I was willingly lost, with the essence of who I could be submerged beneath all the identities that were created for me; not knowing that admitting I was lost was the first step to being found. Instead, I fell deeper into the ever-growing black hole that had become my soul.

The harsh reality of my nothingness came when my marriage fell apart. My husband had been engaged in a relationship with a co-worker for a while before I found out and when the truth emerged, I tried to be okay with it. Yes, be okay with the extra-marital relationship! How crazy was that?! It was so crazy it didn't work and ultimately we finally crashed and burned. As dysfunctional as my marriage was and as unhappy as I was in the dysfunction, dysfunction was all I knew; I clung to it like a warm coat so when my marriage finally imploded I was devastated because I could no longer deny the truth.

I could lie and say my devastation was rooted in the feeling of rejection that bloomed inside me like a flower in the spring; after all, I had been rejected quite a bit throughout my life. However, if there was ever a time to be truthful, this time was as good as any. This latest run in with my nemesis rejection left me in a state of paralysis; like a deer caught in the headlights not knowing what to do or where to go. My husband's absence left a chasm as wide and as deep as the ocean and I was somewhere in that vast void. I didn't have anything or anyone to quickly replace the void and for the first time ever, I was standing face to face with my nothingness staring into a darkness that scared me. I wasn't sure I would survive. I wasn't sure I wanted to.

Suicide. I thought about it. Constantly. It was the first thought I had each day I woke up to the barren desert my life had become and the last thought I had at night after thinking, "I just can't do this again tomorrow". Every day was a struggle worse than the day before and I was losing my resolve to fight. My children were constantly in the forefront of my mind but I was coming to the conclusion that they were better off without me. My inability to disconnect and move beyond all the other tentacles that came with the spirit of rejection was impacting my ability to be a good mother. I was failing them and it was just one more thing that was added to the column of growing reasons why leaving this life could work out for everyone. Yes, suicide was more than a notion. I couldn't run from my thoughts, I couldn't slow them down nor put them on pause. I was trapped and could see no way out.

When someone makes the decision to kill him or herself, it's not because one terrible thing happened. Often times, it's a build-up of hurt, failure, loss, anxiety, rejection, silence, etc., and all it takes is one small thing that occurs and that small thing becomes the proverbial straw to break the camel's back. The same is true in my case; it was nothing epic or noteworthy that occurred. It was a minor exchange of words between my husband and myself when compared to some of our past confrontations. I still don't know why that specific conversation affected me the way it did but it was the one that put me over the edge.

With my mind made up, I left work early. I gave everyone my painted on smile with the already broken promise that I would see them tomorrow; I paused only briefly to thank the receptionist who always looked at me with sage eyes, as she told me she was praying for me. I appreciated the sentiment but I wasn't sure her prayer would get to God in time.

I drove home on autopilot and it was only as I got out of my car that I noticed the bubble of a car sitting in front my house. It was packed to the roof with stuff. I wondered how anyone could fit; but someone did, as the driver got out and started walking towards me. Years later it's still clear in my mind the eccentric looking woman who seemed to float despite her bulky clothing. "Are you Kim?" she asked. I was annoyed; she was interrupting my plan and I grudgingly acknowledge I was Kim. Not deterred by my brusqueness, she said, "Melinda sent me. God wants you to know that it's not your time to die." It was like a dam had been breached. I fell into her arms and just cried. I just couldn't stop. I cried for what seemed like hours and the whole time she just held me and prayed.

Sitting on the curb, I admitted to her my plan to end my life. I couldn't seem to stop the flood of tears that were coming from a place that I thought had long since dried up. She took me to the hospital because she wasn't comfortable leaving me alone. After being checked in they mildly sedated me but in a moment of lucidity, the one scripture that came to my mind was Amos 5:4, "Seek ye me and ye shall live". Those seven words remained an echo in my mind and while there was so much that still wasn't clear, what rung clear was that I was at a crucible moment. I could continue trying to do it my way or I could seek God and find out who I was in Him and do it His way. I had come to the end of myself so I had nothing to lose by beginning again with God.

As I walked out of the hospital that evening, I made a promise to God that I was never coming back to that place. I wasn't talking about the hospital, but I was talking about that dark place that had been home for way too many years. I made a promise to seek him because I really did want to live, even if I didn't know how.

Seeking God required me to learn about Him; I had to read the Word beyond the surface to learn who and why He is. It required me to lean into and on Him. Seeking God required me to develop a prayer life, a life where I not only talked to Him but I listened to Him and developed a spirit of obedience. It required me to not just bend my will but to lay it completely down and pick up His will for my life. The more I sought him, the deeper my relationship with Him became and I found that my identity was found in Him.

Acts 17:28 says, "In Him we live and move and have our being." Your identity is in Christ. Until you know who God is, you won't know who you are. Knowing who you are and understanding why you are, is critical because that knowledge equips you with the ability to reject anything that doesn't line up with God's blueprint for your life. When you're following God's blueprint it frees you from the weight and responsibility of people, tags and titles that sometimes do more to hinder than help you.

When we learn who we are, our entire being transforms and that knowledge dictates who we are as friends, parents, significant others, etc. The truth of who I was convicted me into acknowledging the role I played in the demise of some of the relationships I was party to, especially my marriage. Truth is that stabilizing entity that forces you to see things as they really are, whether you like it or not. Truth made me acknowledge and take responsibility for my role in the train wreck that was my marriage. Acknowledging my role did not negate my husband's role but as I walked through the truth of my transformation, I had to stop blaming my husband for everything and become accountable for my behaviors, that weren't conducive to a healthy marriage. If I didn't know who I was, who was I asking him to love? I had to learn how to be a friend to myself. I had to learn to love me before I could even consider or graciously receive love from anyone else.

Learning to love myself was difficult. Sometimes before we can move forward we have to go back and frequently we're afraid of turning that rock over to see what's on the other side. Digging down to the root cause of everything was a painful process but it was imperative to uncover the rejection, pride, fear and self-actualization that for years silently eroded my self-esteem and confidence. I wanted to be excited about meeting the real me but I had to be delivered from the strongholds that could impede the fragility of new love from taking root. Being a foreigner in your mind, body and spirit is not fertile ground for God-actualization. I was traveling unchartered waters and knew I couldn't navigate the process of repentance on my own.

I had to be deliberate about my salvation and do what wisdom would dictate especially since I was unsure about where I was or what I lost. I asked for directions. I became a member of a bible-teaching ministry, where the leaders were more concerned about my soul than they were my feelings. It was hard but they prayed with me, prayed for me, corrected me in love and kept me accountable to the commitment I made with God. I had never been pushed that far out of my comfort zone before but every time I felt myself ready to give up, I remembered that Jesus went even further for me. I kept in the forefront of my mind that if God saw fit to save me and my spiritual leaders invested the time they did pushing me, the least I could do, was go the extra degree because failure was no longer an option.

Galatians 2:20 says, "I have been crucified with Christ. It is no longer I who live, but Christ who lives in me. And the life I now live in the flesh I live by faith in the Son of God, who loved me and gave himself for me." Deconstructing the old mindset was a daily chore and some days it was harder than others but it was a chore that was necessary if I was going to walk successfully in my salvation. My life was no longer my own and I did not want to devalue the new life that was afforded me through the covenant of repentance and redemption with God. I had to see things through His eyes and fully partake in His wisdom, which governed the way I interacted with everyone. I was seeing everything and everyone through the lens of grace.

My Spiritual Leader at the time, once preached, "In impossibilities, is where true faith and courage rises to the occasion; but when things seem impossible, it guarantees that God is present on the scene". I didn't think it was possible that life could be found amongst the wreckage that was in my life but God had a different plan and submission to Him and His plan for my life was where the possibilities of my life began. I certainly did not think it was possible but I marvel every day at what can happen when you discard your plans in favor for God's plans.

I know you're wondering what happened to my marriage. We tried to put it back together. We tried to recapture what we thought we had with each other but after a while we had to acknowledge that we were now two different people, going in two different directions and we really didn't know the individuals who emerged from the ashes. Did this revelation hurt? It absolutely did! This was the person with whom I had spent the last eighteen years of my life. We couldn't, however, wallow in the loss of each other because we had children that we had nurtured and loved through this transition in an effort to keep them whole. It wasn't easy but we were motivated by a shared love for our children. We had to press through the hurt and sometimes even the anger to do what we knew to be the right thing for them. It was no longer about us, but really about how to show them the love of Christ through our interaction with each other.

I prayed and sought the direction of God, who I now knew to be the source of my strength and a fountain of wisdom and after hearing from Him and seeking counsel from spiritual elders who I trusted and knew wanted the best for all of us, I sat with my husband and created a de-coupling plan that would position all of us, specifically our children, for success as we worked to put our lives back together, albeit separately, and adapt to a new normal. It was hard and challenging at times but forgiveness is an action word that when put in motion, gives life to peace and creates a fertile atmosphere for the fruit of the spirit to grow and flourish!

I am grateful every day that God was the first responder on the scene; I'm grateful He saw beyond my faults and frailties and gave me another opportunity to live out His plan for my life with His guidance through His written Word and the multitude of counselors He sent to encourage, equip and empower me. I've learned that failed marriages or relationships don't have to be filled with angst and acrimony and after coming so close to literally losing my life, I did not want to spend a moment being unforgiving and bitter. It is possible, when you're actively walking in forgiveness and love to be a light that draws others to a life with Christ.

As I reflect on how far I've travelled spiritually, I am now able to look on that day when I came to the end of myself and recognize that for all intent and purpose, I really did die. What emerged from the ashes was something more valuable. I am no longer paralyzed in a state of debilitative anxiety and I don't dwell on those dark days but I always remember the destitute and barren terrain that was my soul. This memory keeps me focused and in a state of facilitative anxiety, which

propels me forward and keeps me focused on where God is taking me. I don't ever want to go back and when you become whole in God, you don't have to.

I am boldly walking in God's purpose for my life; establishing ministry as He directs, teaching and encouraging His people and continuing to be fed spiritually. In God I live, I move and have my being and after so many years of waiting to die, each morning I wake up ready and prepared to live.

SHAKELA STRAWBERRY
Unshackled from Unforgiveness

There are so many disillusions regarding forgiveness, it's definition and how it should be displayed. Unlike some try to make it appear, it's not a simple or complicated scientific $1+1=2$. Forgiveness deals with emotions, reactions, and both internal and external forces. The end result of forgiveness should always be freedom. It is often a constant state of perfecting. Because of this, forgiveness is not a science, but rather an art.

Forgiveness is releasing someone of the guilt and hurt they may have caused you. While it can be the acceptance of an apology, an apology does not have to be given in order for forgiveness to take place. Forgiveness means that you do not hold what happened as an offense over that person. If we read the Parable of the Unmerciful Servant in Matthew 18:21-35, we realize that forgiveness is an extension of mercy.

I was once taught that forgiveness meant to throw things into the sea of forgetfulness. However, as I have matured I have found out that forgiveness is not always forgetting. In some cases, such as the case of a broken joint that is now healed, no matter how the healing takes place one can often feel twinges of pain now and again. This is why in our humanity, offenses, while they can be forgiven, can't always be forgotten. When a bruise is created, the wound may heal, but the scar may remain forever. I have had several surgeries in my life. While I may no longer feel the pain as a direct result of those surgeries, I still see and in some cases feel the scars. However, the scar doesn't always hurt.

So what does it mean to forget it? Let us look to the cross. Jesus saw a thief on the cross in need of salvation. He didn't use what he did wrong against him, rather he saw he needed help and still chose to offer it to him. This is what forgetfulness is about. Once we forgive, we relinquish our right to bring up the offense.

I will never forget as a teenager, someone spoke to me about forgiveness. Someone had really hurt me and I was not sure that I could continue with the relationship even after I forgave the person. They gave me the example of when we were kids and when someone did us wrong we would say that we were not going to be their friend anymore. They explained how it was immature then, and it is the same now and does not show true forgiveness. While the person had great intentions, this definition kept me trapped for years. The main reason for this is because I kept feeling like the relationship had to go back to the way it was and that same person kept committing the same offenses towards me or even worse offenses. Forgiveness does not mean the relationship has to go back to its original state. We do not see Jesus running to those who crucified him when he rose from the dead. However, forgiveness is definitely a spiritual release for both oneself and the offender. I saw this picture a few months ago and it said perfectly how I felt about forgiveness: *Forgiveness is a process just like grief at times and depending on the offense. It doesn't look the same from day to day.*

Any offense against you needs to be forgiven. I have found myself looking at people differently because of how they treated my husband, mother, children, siblings, or friend. Some, I may have approached requesting an apology, while others I just had to pray about and give the scenario and relationship to God.

There is also the story of the Prodigal Son. In Luke 15:11-32, we learn about the son who prostituted his father's grace. For years he did what he knew was wrong even knowing that his actions hurt his father including moving away from him to get away from the accountability. We learn at the end of the story that while the son was ready to apologize to his father for what he had done, his father did not even wait for his apology to greet him, embrace him and celebrate him. Forgiveness had taken place even while the son's heart was still hardened.

The resurrection and the Prodigal son are two different expressions of forgiveness, yet both forgave. The contrast between them explains why forgiveness is an art that is constantly being perfected. There will be some that do us wrong where God will permit the relationship to change. But God's perfecting will is always for reconciliation. This is what I believe that person was trying to teach me so long ago. Unfortunately, human acts and consequences of our actions may not always allow that to be possible in the same manner the relationship was in the beginning. What's the difference? Knowing God's will for your life and your relationship that is affected. Of course, the only ways to really know that is to stay in relationship and communication with Him.

Any offense against you needs to be forgiven. I have found myself looking at people differently because of how they treated my husband, mother, children siblings or friend. Some, I may have approached requesting an apology, while others I just had to pray about and give the scenario and relationship to God. Truthfully, according to the Bible, they all should have been approached regardless of the end status of that relationship. God always want us to turn every situation and relationship over to Him.

As I reflected on the many lessons of forgiveness I have learned, I realized that all of my mentors have one thing in common: they have all hurt me in some aspect that required my forgiveness. One mentor in particular I was extremely angry with him to the point that I did not go to minister to him on his deathbed, as I could not even look at him. It took me a couple of weeks to get myself together to go and speak to him and accept his apology. The day that I had purposed to go and see him, he passed away before I could get there. I cried not because of grief, but I cried because I was angry with myself for not seeing him sooner. I cried because I wondered what would happen if God did the same to me. I cried and I remembered how Jesus, while on the cross, offered forgiveness for His offenders. That day, I'd made up in my mind two things: 1) Forgiveness should be immediate and 2) There is never a time when forgiveness should not be offered. If Jesus could forgive those that persecuted him, there is nothing that is unforgiveable. Perhaps one of the reasons I didn't think so in the past is because I believed I had to forget, let go, and feel the same way about the person that I did pre-offense. I have found that is simply not the case. Just as love is a process that grows, forgiveness, which is an extension of love, also grows.

I have been adamant about teaching my children to forgive right away. Yet, there is a process and that process should be respected. Due to my past experiences, I want to dispel the myth that to forgive someone means to let them know "It's okay". My children are required to forgive right away, they are forbidden to say, "It's okay". The conversation goes like: "I'm sorry _____." Immediate Response: "I forgive you". The response in my home is required to be immediate just as Jesus on the cross, but the response is forbidden to be "It's okay". The reason for this is because the broken plate will NEVER be the same. It was hurt, and that is not okay. It is not okay that it will never be the way it was. There will forever be cracks even if the cracks are hard to see. This is also the reason that relationships cannot always be put back together; or if they are, have grooves where you can feel and see the brokenness.

The goal of forgiveness is healing a release for the person offended. If there is a relational aspect to forgiveness (like my children forgiving each other or a friend forgiving the other) it can also be a release and healing for the offender. I correlate it so close with grief because when someone offends you it is similar to a death depending on the relationship. Forgiveness is a part of the reflection or can be part of the reconstruction phase of grief and in different stages of the forgiveness. For some relationships it is simply part of the reflection and the acceptance is that the relationship will never be the same. For those who are trying to push pass, there is one stage of forgiveness at the reflection stage and a level of maturing forgiveness at the reconstruction phase of forgiveness/grief.

As I stated above, I have had several mentors in my life, but a common thread with every last one of them is that they have severely fallen short in some area or another and all have hurt me deeply at some point. Some people wonder how then can they be your mentors if they have hurt you. I have learned that no one is perfect. I have also learned that the only way they can hurt me so deep is for me to have a deep love and respect for them. If they don't hold a special place in my heart, then it really doesn't affect me as much. In my humanity, I also remember that I too have disappointed people. I too have let people down, even if that was not my intention. I too have had times where I just wanted to be selfish and not have to worry about how my actions affected another. I remember what forgiveness looks like on the cross. I recall Jesus saying, "forgive them, for they know not what they do". I remember that He said that on the cross, in the midst of being wronged. I find it ironic how He did not wait until His resurrection, I mean He knew He would rise and that He had time, but He chose to do it in the midst of persecution.

While I know that forgiveness (especially for certain

things that are egregious) is a process, I know now that I have the power to release that person (forgive them) in the midst of the wrong and allow the total healing process to take place.

Forgiveness is love. A mature developed love does not look the same as newfound love. It doesn't make the newfound love a less love; it just makes it less developed. I told my husband twenty years ago that I loved him and truly meant it, but after twenty-one years of being together, it means even more and has so much more depth to it. When you first forgive someone, depending on the offense it may look different from the beginning of the process to the end. This is why some relationships can be mended and some must be severed.

During another time on the cross, Jesus asked his Father to *forgive them, as they did not know what they were doing*. Once again, He saw a need for mercy and to save their souls from damnation, He not only forgave them, but requested God forgive them as well. Can you be the one that fulfills their need? Can you look pass what they did to you and see them through the cross enough to assist them if they needed it? Isn't that what Jesus did for us? While we were yet sinners, He died for us.

How will you look at forgiveness given the example Jesus gave us on the cross? Have you been doing things to trap you and hinder you from healing from those that have offended you sincerely thinking that you have forgiven that person? Have you forgiven yourself for any offenses that may be eating away at you? Remember that just like love and grief, forgiveness is not a "quick fix". It is not something you say and magically it is true. Work follows. Spirit still follows. Most importantly, the process still follows. As long as you walk through the process and let the process take its course, you will find the barriers broken and the peace within to truly say, "Father forgive them". You, too, can perfect the art of forgiveness.

BARBARA MACK
Unshackled from Cancer

The C word, the dreaded C word. Cancer. A word that turns peoples' lives upside down. A word that causes so much fear and pain. A word that makes people want to give up on life; people decree, I'm going to die. Not so, cancer does not mean a death sentence at all. Because it isn't over until GOD say's it's over.

I am not a medical expert, but having gone through breast cancer twice, I can tell you my truth. Sometimes in our lives, things happen to us to get our attention. Some things happen to make you strong. Moreover, some things happen to get the attention of our loved ones. Either way, there's a lesson to be learned by someone.

I found out Jesus makes the difference in our lives. Man can say there is no hope. Man can say nothing more can be done and walk away, because he has no power. Yet Jesus can always say yes because He has all power. If Jesus does not change the situations in your life, it's not because He can't.

My story begins in October of 2001. I discovered a red spot on the top of my left breast. I showed it to my husband and he said go to the doctor. I went to my primary care doctor. He examined me and thought it was just fatty tissue. He sent me to a surgeon. When the surgeon examined me he said I needed a biopsy. I had the biopsy done the next week. I was still thinking it was fatty tissue. To my surprise, after waiting anxiously for two weeks for the results, the doctor informed me I had cancer. I thought this is not right. This is not for me. Guess what, it was cancer and it was for me and I had to deal with it. This was my time to go through, whether I liked it or not. I had to put my trust in God.

One of the hardest things I had to do was tell my family. I had kept things to myself as long as I could. Now I had to convince them I was going to be alright. God has a way of strengthening you when you need it. My family needed me to encourage them, when I was the one going through. I thank God for His grace and mercy in my life. I never would had made it without Him. Glory to His name!

God started proving Himself to me on October 31, 2001. I was nervous, anxious, fearful, not really knowing what to expect. I had questions with no answers. What would they find? Had the cancer spread to another part of my body? I had been praying. I could not find the peace I needed to go into surgery. About 1:30 a.m., as I was lying down to sleep, I glanced at the head of my bed. I saw the words that changed my way of thinking forever. *Fear not, for I am with you. Be not dismayed for I am your God. I will strengthen you; yes I will help you. I will uphold you with my righteous right hand.* My God, I got so excited, I jumped up and ran to the other room to tell my daughter, but she was asleep. I tried to tell my husband, but he too was asleep. I was about to burst. I wanted to tell someone. I needed to tell it! God is with me! There was no one I could call at that hour. Then I realized the words were for me only. I had to digest God's words all by myself.

What a mighty God we serve. This was my answer, I thought. I reread the words over and over again as I cried tears of joy. I knew then all was well. No more need to fear, because I had the reassurance of my God. I was in His hands, He had my back, and there was nothing to fear at all. You know, even until this day, when I get down and out, I go to my Bible and I read Isaiah 41: 9 – 10. These words always lift my spirit, knowing God is with me always.

Six o'clock that morning I was admitted to the hospital for the lumpectomy of my left breast. I thank God they did not have to take the whole breast. I went into surgery surrounded by family and loved ones. I prayed with them, and I was fearless and full of peace. I had nothing to worry about. I trusted and believed the Word of God. All was well.

They told me after surgery I would be in a lot of pain. I was given a pain pump and told to keep pushing the button. When the nurse came in the next day, to her surprise, I had not pushed the button, not once. When she asked why, I confessed that I had no pain at all. The nurses' eyes got as big as saucers. She couldn't believe it. God was working it out for me. I only had to spend one night in the hospital. Praise God!

The doctors informed me they had gotten all of the cancer, but I would still need to take chemotherapy and radiation. Being fifty-three years old and the size of the tumor, they thought the cancer would come back. The doctor put me on daily pills for ten years, supposedly to keep the cancer from coming back. As you will see, the pills did not work for me. Everything about the surgery went according to the doctor's plan; I was ready for my next treatments.

It was chemotherapy time and I had to learn about the process. I was given books and pamphlets to read. As I read the horror stories concerning the after effects of chemotherapy, I was again filled with fear and dread. I did not want any part of it. I told the doctor I was not going to take it. I just can't go through all of that. "You have to if you want to live", he said. I left there determined I would not take chemotherapy for anybody. I knew they couldn't make me if I refused.

Do you see how fast we forget? How fast we can change our minds? I believed all the stories. I took in all the pain and suffering and made it my own. I could fell it for real. One night while reading, I couldn't move my legs. It was sad. I had forgotten about the word of God and how He had promised to be with me. I only thought of the negative things associated with chemotherapy. Some shackles had already been broken. How could I forget?

One afternoon, I received a call from my niece. Still down about the chemotherapy, I started to tell her how I was feeling about things. I told her what the doctors told me. Then I found myself telling her how God brought me through the surgery pain free. How He told me I was in His hands. I got so excited telling her about the goodness of God and what God had already done for me. My niece said it seems like you have already made up your mind. I laughed and said I have. Just thinking of the goodness of God and what He had already done brought me back to reality and my mind was made up. I trusted God, and there was nothing I couldn't go through with Him.

I took my first chemotherapy treatment out of four on December 6, 2001. I went with a little bit of nervousness. I really didn't know what to expect. My daughter and brother were with me and they too were nervous. Everybody was very quiet. We were surprised when they took us to a room that had a recliner and television in it. I had a port in the right side of my chest for the infusion. I was ready to go. The treatment lasted for four hours. I went home waiting for the side effects to begin. Glory to God, I never got sick from the treatments. I didn't lose weight. I was tired a lot, and I couldn't taste most foods, but I was able to eat what I wanted. After my second treatment I lost all of my hair. That was the hardest thing for me. They told me I would, but I was hoping not. I thank God for wigs. Wigs became my friend until my hair grew back.

Things began to get really personal between God and me while I was going through my treatments. I had problems sleeping at night. I slept great in the mornings. I had my days and nights mixed up. We all know that an idle mind is the devils workshop. The enemy started talking to my mind. He comes to steal, kill, and destroy God's people. Since I was weak and tired, I had a pity party. I was thinking very negative things. No one's thinking about me. This one hasn't been to see me, that one hasn't called me. Why doesn't somebody care? I was in a state; *a "why me"* *state*. One night God spoke to me and said, "Don't worry about the ones who don't, praise Me for the ones that do. I am with you always. I won't leave you or forsake you. Trust Me in all things". I will never forget those words. Another shackle has been broken.

You know I think sometimes how can you be surrounded by people when things are going well, but when you are going through, family and friends seem to disappear. I thank God for His presence in my life. My chemotherapy days and nights took on new meaning when I accepted what God allowed and realized it was all about Him and not about me. Another shackle gone!

On March 19, 2002, I began my thirty-two radiation treatments. I went five days a week. I was able to drive myself every day. God was still with me. There were no problems with the radiation treatments. The treatment lasted about fifteen minutes, and I was on my way.

Life got back to normal. I visited my oncologist and radiation doctors routinely after my treatments were completed. Five years later, while being examined by the radiation doctor, she found a lump in my right breast. She ordered a mammogram. The tech said it's not cancer. I was sent to another surgeon who did a biopsy in his office. This was December 29, 2005. I went back for the results two weeks later to hear the surgeon say, Mrs. Mack you have cancer. I was shocked. I could only say okay. He sent me to my oncologist that same afternoon. As my husband and I walked to the car, I told him the cancer was back. While sitting in the car I called a girl friend of mine, she said it's not cancer is it? I said yes it is. She was shocked. I broke down crying and when I looked up my husband was crying also. Do you know what? That was the first and last time I shed a tear.

This tumor was larger than the first. The oncologist wanted to remove the breast. He asked, "you don't want that do you?" I said no, so he called in another doctor. She looked at the X rays and suggested trying to shrink the tumor first. He agreed to try shrinking the tumor first. On February 24, 2006, I started my first chemotherapy treatment out of four. After my second treatment, during an examination of my breast, the doctor could not find the tumor. Another doctor was called in to examine me. He found no tumor. The tumor was gone, gone, gone. It had just disappeared. The doctor said they had never had a patient's tumor disappear after two treatments. He told me someone was looking out for me. I said yes, Jesus was looking out for me. Look at God. When you put your trust in God, He will not let you down. People don't believe in miracles anymore, but with God all things are possible. I was not expecting a miracle, but I thank God He thought me worthy to receive favor, favor, favor. To God be the Glory!

On June 8, 2006, I took my first radiation treatment out of twenty-seven. These were like the first time around except I had gone back to work. I left work every day and drove myself to the treatment center. God had done it again.

I went through breast cancer twice, once in each breast. The ordeal was one I will never forget. The first time was a battle of the mind for me. God had to straighten out some things for me. I found out just how strong my faith was. I found out I couldn't make it without God. When the second bout came it was a new ballgame. God had brought me through the first time and I knew all I had to do was trust Him. To my surprise, there was nothing to go through. It was like I was not going through chemotherapy and radiation. Life was normal for me. I lost my hair, but that was okay too, I had my wigs. It was amazing to me. Working, taking treatments, going where I wanted, doing things I wanted to do. What a mighty God we serve!

My daughter asked me why God allowed me to have cancer the second time when I was not sick or going through anything. You know I thought about it for a while before I answered, "God has a purpose and a reason for everything He allows us to go through. We may not see it or understand it, but there is something for you or someone else to see or to get out of it. It's not always about us. It's not about who. It's not about what we've done or not done. He sees all and knows all. I found out what's for you is for you only. We have to know God makes no mistakes. God is in charge of our lives and He has no respecter of persons. What He does for others, He'll do the same for you. God loves us with an everlasting love. When we love God and one another unconditionally, when we trust and believe God with our whole heart, when we are willing to give up the wrong for the right, our lives will change for the better. It is then the shackles in our lives can be broken forever.

By the way, I have been cancer free in my left breast for fifteen years now. I have been cancer free in my right breast for ten years now. To God be the Glory!

JOYCE SAMUELS
Unshackled from Abuse

On June 21, 2007, I began to write a journal after many nights of prompting and pushing from my inner being. I had put off writing a book about my life for many, many years. Yet, after much consideration and after so many late night "wake up" calls, I have given in to at least begin to write about my childhood. Whatever comes out of this, well, then, it is what it is!

My attitude is, it is time to tell my story; one because it really is therapeutic for me and two, there are so many girls, and young women who have either gone through or are experiencing the embarrassment, pain, humiliation and agonizing sufferings that have torn and haunted them for years. I want them to know that I am a survivor of abuse by women. Very seldom do you know of women on women abuse, but it is real and it does happen. It's rare that you hear of women raping other women, but it happens daily and the scars are even worse than what men do to women or little girls because no one can see the evidence. No one ever speaks about how there are real demented females who have raped or are raping innocent young ladies. How do you prove that? How do you prove that a long hard object was thrust up my vagina? How do you prove that fingers and tongues were used in places that were not supposed to be. My proof is my inner scars, physically and emotionally. My proof is my secret, quiet attempts of suicide, my late night demon attacks and the main outcome of this abuse is my lack of trust of all women. Yes, the struggle is real and God is still working on and in me every day to get past this inner hurt and scars.

The story begins with my biological mother. It is difficult to try to remember every small detail of my childhood life from the age of 12 and earlier. However, the most I do remember about my life was when I was removed from my grandmother's home (my biological father's mother) at the tender age of five almost six years old. I remember being tossed to and fro; from one relative's home to the next, and I know that was not unusual for most families, especially in the sixties and seventies.

I remember my mother being drunk or high on something almost every day and night. She had different men and women coming in and out of our home whenever my siblings and I did live with her. It seemed like we always had a party! There was a time when I was maybe about four years old and my mother and father had just come back from the bar. They were both very drunk, of course, staggering, slurring and cussing. My older brothers and sisters who had just come in from off the streets were trying to keep us younger ones away from them. A huge fight broke out; I mean it was bad. They started fighting over who was going to leave, who was going to stay and who was going to take which child with whom. The fight lasted for hours. My younger brothers and I were so scared that we couldn't even sleep that night. We lay under the bed, with our eyes closed tightly shut and our hands over our ears. I was terrified and I remember having to go to the bathroom, but didn't want to move. I was so afraid to say anything so I just let urine run down my leg. I lay in that urine all night. When morning came, my oldest sister was livid. She smacked me so hard I saw red dots. I wasn't mad though. I understood her frustration, pain, and anguish. After all, she was the only "mother" I really knew. She finally let us come out of hiding. Of course, the house was a complete disaster. Our father was gone, and our mother was passed out on the partial couch. Clothes, pieces of furniture, towels, alcohol and food were thrown everywhere. We even saw stains of blood on the carpet. My two older sisters didn't say a word. They just went to work. One started cleaning the house; the other started cleaning the three of us younger ones. I can't express how grateful I was to have my oldest sister. She took a lot of the abuse for our sakes. She literally cared for my three younger brothers and me every day. She made sure that we were fed and put on fresh clothes. Even though we had no running water most of the time or even soap to wash with, she still made us clean. One time she washed us in spoiled milk. It smelled horrible, but at least we were clean, right? We never had food in the house. Never!

Whenever it was time for us to eat, my older siblings would rummage through trashcans in the alley to find us a half-eaten burger, a chewed up steak or just a chicken bone. There was a time that we were so hungry but the only thing we had in the little shack was about half box of generic cereal. My sisters poured the cereal in a cake pan, grabbed a wooden serving spoon with holes in it, poured water over the cereal and fed us one by one. She made sure we all had a spoonful. She passed it around about three times and then she took the last bite. Just thinking about that time brings tears to my eyes. We were still hungry after that so she promised when she returned that evening, that we would have a meal. And she did not disappoint. We ate well that night. I don't know what she did or how she did it, but she brought back some chicken thighs and bread. By that evening, my mother was sober enough to fix us a meal. My mother could cook very well. Even though it was rare. Most times, the only occasion I recall ever seeing our mother was when she was passed out in bed or lying on the couch with another man in her arms. My mother was so beautiful. But it was not often we were able to experience her beauty due to her seeking love and attention through men, alcohol and drugs. She was a totally different person when she was "cleaned" up.

It didn't last long, maybe a few days here or there. Yet she was lovable and nurturing then. She would teach us how to cook and make us clean ourselves. She showed the older siblings how to hustle for food and water from our neighbors. I really enjoyed those days. She treated us like her children, would call us little pet names and make our hair so pretty. We all cherished those days. She played lots of music and loved to dance and sing to us. It was strange at first because it was so rare that we did not know how to accept her when she was happy. It just never lasted long. As soon as one of her special friends came by and flashed money or booze and empty promises in her face, she would become another woman. We wouldn't see her for days. She let many things happen to us. Many things. That's when my world became dark and cold and lonely. I was so lonely. We had so many people coming in and out. Bad people. Dirty people. Nasty people. These people, mainly women, did horrible things to us that you wouldn't even do to an animal. We were tortured, burned, raped, molested repeatedly. Mostly us girls were attacked because we were the only ones home. They would watch us squirm and bleed and laugh when we begged them to stop. I remember my sister screaming and pleading for one particular couple to stop. They took turns being on top of her. She came in to save me from them and sacrificed herself instead. I hid in the closet behind old musty clothes while she just let them torture her. She kept looking over her shoulder at me and motioned for me to close my eyes. I couldn't stand it. I don't know how she survived. I believe she was only eleven at the time. I believe after the incident she ran away, or at least I didn't see her again until she came to visit my younger siblings and me in our foster home. She turned to the streets and was heavy on drugs for years. I can truly understand. Can't judge her. I buried her at the tender age of 30. A few months later, we had to bury her two sons one four years old and the other four months old. They all died of AIDS.

For years I blamed my mother. Didn't she hear our cries for help? Didn't she care? Why did she let them hurt us? Where was my beautiful, caring, cooking mother? Why didn't she save us?

It even got so bad that our half-brother and sometimes our cousins came over to have sex with each other. My oldest sister stayed around as long as she could before the state came and took her away. Once that happened, you can imagine what was being done to me. I was the only girl left. Word got around that there were younger children in our home with no supervision and our grandmother came and got us for a period of time. She was way too old to care for us, but she tried. My oldest sister came back to get us one time. She was emancipated by then. Not sure how we all ended up back on the streets though. By this time, I was about five or six. There were a total of eight children. Two older brothers had different fathers. By the time my sister came back into our lives, only four of us were around to go with her. We stayed from house to house. I don't recall how we all got separated, but we were scattered. My younger brother and I ended up with our two middle siblings. They were very street smart. And could run very fast. Somehow we ended up on the streets, living out of a cardboard box house and just other boxes and newspaper to cover us up with. We dug out of trashcans again to eat, many nights just sucking the mare out of the bone. My older siblings would steal bread off the Sunbeam bread truck around 4:00 a.m. every day. Times got very hard. We fought off robbers, muggers, rapist, molesters and other homeless people to survive. I shake my head in amazement. Only God could have gotten us out of that. Only God.

Finally our grandmother came back and got us yet again. My

younger siblings and I ended up in foster homes. I never saw my two middle aged siblings again until years later.

I tell you all of this because I survived. Despite the fact that everyone said that we were all no good and we were going to end up like my mother, who died at the age of 41. Furthermore, despite the fact that two of my siblings who witnessed the most pain and suffering died younger than that, I can attest of God's grace. I still don't understand how and I dare not ask why, all I know is that God has allowed me to live to tell the story. I lived to tell you that no matter what has happened to you in your past, you can overcome anything. You may be the one reading this right now and recognize you were the one who gave your child up for adoption or you caused harm on many people from your past and you may think that you can't be forgiven. Not so. You can still overcome. Let God break that shackle!

You may be the one reading this story about my life and old painful scars resurface from your childhood and you think that you will never be able to forgive the ones who caused this on you. Well, not so! For years I walked around angry. I didn't even want to talk about my past. I was so broken. I was lost and I was dying inside. Yes, I was singing with the choir, but dying. I was shouting and dancing in church, but still dying. I would preach and teach to many and talk about forgiveness but was not living accordingly. Basically I was living a lie! I was allowing the shackles of my past to control my future.

Finally, when I began to write this, the pain became real. I had to find and contact many family members to find out who I was. I accepted the fact that even though I tried to hide behind my smile, I was still hurting. I was still that little girl who hid in the closet behind those musty clothes witnessing a horrific act on my dear sister. I was still that little girl who hid under the bed, wet, cold and scared of my own parents due to the violent behavior. I wanted to yell, scream and spit in their face. I blamed them for everything. Yet, when I finally allowed God to let me see them through His eyes, I realized that they did the best that they knew how. I had to forgive them even if they never asked for it. It was too late for my mother to tell me what pain she went through during those times. She died a terrible death, but I lived to tell the story. I was raped, but I lived to tell the story. I was abused, but I lived to tell the story. I was molested, but I lived to tell the story! The chains are falling off day by day.

So my dear sisters and brothers, who may be reading this right now, if you feel like giving up, please don't! Learn to walk in forgiveness. Ask God to forgive you. Don't hold up your breakthrough by not walking in love. Don't hold up your victory by not learning how to forgive. I survived and so can you. Forgive yourself, then let go of your shackles!!!

ABOUT THE AUTHORS

Sharron Peterson is a native Washingtonian. She was raised by her single mother, Claudette Allen and is the oldest of four other siblings.

Sharron received her Medical Certification at Walter Reed Army Medical Center in Washington, District of Columbia and has served in the medical field for over twenty years.

Sharron believes in family and is loved by her large family members. Many know her to be a kind, generous and a loving giver like her mother was.

She's a survivor and a faith walker and she is grateful that God turned her test into a testimony to help others see what God can bring you out of.

Sharron's favorite past time is attending church, traveling, cooking and spending quality time with her three children. She loves to minister to the youth about Jesus.

Minister Valerie Johnson-Philson was born to Minister Barbara Johnson-Mack and Edward Johnson. She has a younger sister. She is married to Craig Philson, and has four children (Craig, Lucretia, Edward and Daniel) and six grandchildren (Remia, Saiya, Jaylen, Destiny, D'Marco and Ja'liya). She has worked for Housing and Urban Development for 14 years and is currently a GS-13 Administrative Management Specialist.

Valerie serves as a Minister in training at Praise Redemption Worship Center, under the leadership of Bishop Nathaniel Huggins.

She began her Christian college education at Washington Bible College in June 2010. She graduated from Lancaster Bible College in August 2014, with a BA in Business Administration. She is currently attending Capital Seminary pursuing a Master's degree in Leadership.

Minister Linda D. Parker was born to Mr. & Mrs. Joseph Beavers. To this union, she is the youngest of twelve children. Linda's parents inspired her to be the woman of God she is today. Currently she attends Rising Star Holy Temple under the leadership of Pastor James M. Hillian and has traveled teaching and preaching the gospel.

Minister Linda has been in the medical field caring for the elderly for over 18 years. She enjoys this and considers this her full time ministry.

Another one of her enjoyment are her three children, six grandchildren and one great grand.

Her favorite past time is reading and studying the Word of God.

Yvonne Lovelady is an ordained Evangelist, teacher and high school track coach. She has four children who are now independently supporting themselves.

Yvonne is the founder of Love & Care Outreach International Ministry, a ministry that feeds and clothes the homeless. Since she was nine years old, Yvonne has had a special passion to feed and encourage others. Yvonne loves to encourage and feed those who are less fortunate, letting them know they are not forgotten. In her spare time, she volunteers at various soup kitchens in the Lake County area of Illinois

Chikita Brown Mann has as over 22 years of experience in the healthcare profession as a nurse case manager. Her writing experience has been in creating continuing education courses. She has a wonderful husband with three beautiful children, one daughter and 2 sons.

After an encounter with the Lord, she understood her calling to bring awareness to others of the correlation between one's spiritual health and physical health. Chikita is the health and fitness coordinator at Covenant Christian Ministries in Marietta, GA. She also serves as a Commissioner with the Commission for Case Management Certification.

Tiffany L. Johnson is the founder and owner of *Voice To Perfection,* a voice media service. She has been heard on major radio and television networks across the nation such as Black Entertainment Television, Inc. now owned by CBS/Viacom, the Bay Radio Station in Southern Maryland; Bay Vision Cable Television News Station and Metro Networks, and a news service provider for radio stations throughout the Washington, DC Metropolitan area.

Tiffany has a passion for encouraging women to help them become the best they can be through the help of God. Tiffany also has a passion for writing and telling stories to help inspire women of all walks of life. Tiffany currently works as an Executive Assistant to the Lead Pastors of Metro Church located in the Washington, DC Metropolitan area.

She is a graduate of New York Institute of Technology and holds a Bachelor of Arts Degree in Mass Communications.

Apostle Kim A. DiStefano
Founder of New Covenant Global Alliance

Born in Barbados, West Indies, Kim A. DiStefano is the founder of New Covenant Global Alliance, a ministry birthed to provide radical, unconventional and transformative training and development to equip current and emerging leaders with biblically sound tools and principles necessary to build effective ministries and lead others from religion to relationship with Christ.

With a heart for people and a passion for women's empowerment, Kim was raised up and trained at Kingdom Nation Ministries under the leadership of Apostle Kevin and Lady April Whitson. Her passion and love for God comes from truly being born again and her conviction that only God can transform people and their lives to enable them to realize and reach their God-given purpose.

Apostle Kimberly is also the founder of The Deborah *MOVEMENT*, which started as a dance ministry and evolved into a non-profit organization dedicated to building a network of spiritually- enlightened and empowered women through radical and Christ-centered *MOVEMENT* (**M**inistry, **O**bedience, **V**ision, **E**ducation, **M**otivation, **E**xcellence, **N**etworking and **T**ransformation.

Undoubtedly, her anointing is to assist with establishing market-place ministry and ministering to women according to the Word and will of God. She believes that we are most like Christ when we are in service to others. An accomplished and results oriented consultant and master facilitator with over 15 years of experience working with individuals, teams, and executives, creating vision and structure where there is none and developing end-to-end human resources solutions. Apostle Kim is the President/CEO of Oracle HR Consulting Group, a human resource management consulting firm. She has been a valued advisor and business partner across a broad range of industries.

Apostle Kim is committed to learning and growing in Christ so she can better reach people of all ethnicities. As a teacher of the gospel, her contributions to ministry and to the community have been invaluable and definitely kingdom-building. She is a co-author of, *"Finding Your Voice: The Valley Experience"* and is currently completing her solo project, *"Leading Spiritually in a Volatile, Uncertain, Complex and Ambiguous Environment"*. She is the mother of two children, Shannon (21) and Nathaniel (13). When she is not running her company, being a mother and serving in ministry, Kim serves as a mentor for the 6th Grade Class at Norwood View Elementary School in Cincinnati, OH and is an active advocate for equal education opportunities for all children, in her son's school district. She is an avid reader, loves extreme sports and watching The First 48.

Shakela Strawberry gave her life to the LORD at the tender age of eight. Always knowing she was called to leadership, Shakela answered the call to ministry at the age of 17 when she was licensed to preach by the late Rev. JR McCullough at the Community Baptist Church of Philadelphia. She went on to complete her Bachelor of Arts degree with a dual major in Biblical Studies and Theology at Eastern University. Her ministry includes youth, women, and education. Shakela has been an entrepreneur since 2009 when she leaped into the Real Estate Business. Even in business and vocation, she has a heart for God's people. Her ultimate goal is to assist them in realizing and obtaining the potential God has placed in them. For this reason she went back to school to obtain her Master's Degree in Organizational Leadership. Shakela lives by two mottos: "The devil is busy, but so is God" and "Don't make your reasons your excuses".

Minister Barbara Mack was born in Washington, D.C. and educated in the D.C. public school system. She has been married to a wonderful man, Dennis Mack, for twenty years and they are the loving parents of four wonderful children, nine grandchildren, nine great-grandchildren, and one great-great-grand child.

Minister Barbara is well known for her faithful prayer life and many call her a true Prayer Warrior. She is a licensed Minister at Rising Star Holy Temple in Chapel Oaks, MD. She loves God and God's people. Barbara continues to stand on the scripture, Philippians 3:14. "I press toward the goal for the prize of the upward call of God in Christ Jesus." She realizes the race is not given to the swift or the strong, but to him who endures to the end.

Minister Barbara has completed a certificate course in Biblical Studies and Christian Ministries. She also has a desire to continue to grow stronger in the Lord, to teach, and help God's people.

"Whoever dwells in the shelter of the Most High will rest in the shadow of the Almighty. [2] I will say of the LORD, "He is my refuge and my fortress, my God, in whom I trust."
Psalm 91:1-2

Elder Joyce Samuels, founder of the *JMHS Ministries and the Powerful Prophetic Kingdomites (PPK's)*, is a devoted and dynamic woman of God who strives to encourage, equip, and empower others through the wisdom of Jesus Christ and the power of prayer. She has overcome many childhood obstacles, disappointments and trials that led her to be an advocate for children, an educator, and motivator by enhancing the intellectual and spiritual capacity of others. Elder Samuels has demonstrated her commitment to education naturally and spiritually, with a degree in Education and a medical certification. She was the proprietress of a childcare center and pre-school for 23 years and a principal for 4 years.

Elder Samuels, spiritually birthed under the leadership of Chief Apostle Lannice L. and Apostle Heather D. Collins of Kingdom Covenant International Fellowship of Churches, is licensed and ordained as an Elder and Prophetess with certifications in leadership and mentorship. She and her family recently submitted under the Divine Leadership of Apostle Phyllis Glascoe and Bishop Cordell Glascoe of Shachah World Ministries.

Elder Samuels is energized and excited by the endless opportunities to spread the gospel and share God's love. Her greatest joy is to help people in need. She believes that we are most like Christ when we are in service. She has a heart for all people and operates in God's wisdom to cultivate a love of self, community and service in children, women and men. She aligns herself with the voice of God, to serve and meet the needs of people, spiritually and emotionally. As part of her evangelistic effort, she leads an empowering and Holy Ghost infused *Clarion Prayer Call* each Wednesday mornings at 6:30 a.m.

Elder Samuels has a desire to reach all souls, regardless of ethnicity, gender or generation and is an exemplification of a miracle and survivor. As the literary lead and co-author of the inspirational book, *"Rescued for His Glory: Stories of Hope, Triumph and Wholeness",* she brought together 16 women from across the nation to share their testimonies, in an attempt to have transparent dialogue about the life issues we encounter but suffer silently through. It was a groundbreaking and successful endeavor that created solid spiritual relationships among the women who participated and many of the men and women who read and could see themselves in the shared testimonies. Her most recent literary endeavors, *"Finding Your Voice: The Valley*

Experience" and "Unshackled", promises to be another groundbreaking encounter with God for all who takes the journey with the participating authors.

Elder Samuels is a loving and devoted wife and mother to her husband, Deacon Keith D. Samuels, Sr. and her five (5) children. She is widely known for her powerful prayer life and the gift of faith which fuels her desire to continue learning and growing in Christ so she can continue to teach the truth of the Gospel for the sole purpose of winning souls to the Kingdom. Her current endeavor is returning back to school to pursue a Master's Degree in Psychology.

www.ingramcontent.com/pod-product-compliance
Lightning Source LLC
Chambersburg PA
CBHW060121050426
42448CB00010B/1971